Bre

Thank you for your willingness to follow the direction of the Lord. This weekend was perfectly what I needed!

God is so good :)

Love,
Amy Priddy ♡

Philippians 4:13

JOURNALING THROUGH THE NEW TESTAMENT

Amy Priddy

WESTBOW
PRESS®
A DIVISION OF THOMAS NELSON
& ZONDERVAN

Copyright © 2018 Amy Priddy.

All rights reserved. No part of this book may be used or reproduced by any means, graphic, electronic, or mechanical, including photocopying, recording, taping or by any information storage retrieval system without the written permission of the author except in the case of brief quotations embodied in critical articles and reviews.

Unless otherwise indicated, all Scripture quotations are taken from THE MESSAGE, copyright © 1993, 1994, 1995, 1996, 2000, 2001, 2002 by Eugene H. Peterson. Used by permission of NavPress. All rights reserved. Represented by Tyndale House Publishers, Inc.

Scripture quotations marked (NLT) are taken from the Holy Bible, New Living Translation, copyright ©1996, 2004, 2015 by Tyndale House Foundation. Used by permission of Tyndale House Publishers, Inc., Carol Stream, Illinois 60188. All rights reserved.

Scripture quotations marked (KJV) are taken from the King James Version of the Bible.

WestBow Press books may be ordered through booksellers or by contacting:

WestBow Press
A Division of Thomas Nelson & Zondervan
1663 Liberty Drive
Bloomington, IN 47403
www.westbowpress.com
1 (866) 928-1240

Because of the dynamic nature of the Internet, any web addresses or links contained in this book may have changed since publication and may no longer be valid. The views expressed in this work are solely those of the author and do not necessarily reflect the views of the publisher, and the publisher hereby disclaims any responsibility for them.

Any people depicted in stock imagery provided by Getty Images are models, and such images are being used for illustrative purposes only. Certain stock imagery © Getty Images.

ISBN: 978-1-9736-3935-0 (sc)
ISBN: 978-1-9736-3934-3 (hc)
ISBN: 978-1-9736-3936-7 (e)

Library of Congress Control Number: 2018910807

Print information available on the last page.

WestBow Press rev. date: 09/26/2018

PREFACE

All Scripture is inspired by God and is useful to teach us what is true and to make us realize what is wrong in our lives. It corrects us when we are wrong and teaches us to do what is right. God uses it to prepare and equip his people to do every good work.

—2 Timothy 3:16-17 (NLT)

For the word of God is alive and powerful. It is sharper than the sharpest two-edged sword, cutting between soul and spirit, between joint and marrow. It exposes our inner most thoughts and desires.

—Hebrews 4:12 (NLT)

The Bible is precious to me. Since I was a young girl, I have loved the Bible. I can still remember receiving a Bible for Christmas when I was six years old. I treasure that Bible to this day because it marks the beginning of a lifetime of reading God's love letter to me.

Not only do I enjoy receiving Bibles, but I also love to give Bibles as gifts. One of my favorite gifts to a bride-to-be is a Bible embossed with her new married name. However, a Bible sitting on a shelf holds no more power than any other book. The Bible needs to be read in order to benefit the owner.

Many times, people avoid reading the Bible because the old English language of the King James Version confuses them; or some people only read God's Word when accompanied by a minister or pastor; and others have said it's boring and outdated. It's my desire and hope to encourage people of all ages to pick up their Bibles and read, and not just to check off a list "to be a good Christian," but to realize these words are inspired by God. Our heavenly Father preserved a record of His love for us throughout these pages. This is no ordinary read. These words will change you, if you choose to allow them to.

Journaling through the New Testament contains some of my favorite New Testament passages accompanied by my thoughts. I encourage you to read slowly, one entry per day, and meditate that day upon God's word. The following day, I have provided prompts for you to help you record what the Lord speaks into your spirit. I trust this will be the beginning of a lifestyle of spending time in the presence of God.

> Then Joseph her husband, being a just man, and not willing to make her a public example, was minded to put her away privily.
>
> —Matthew 1:19 (KJV)

What does it mean to be espoused? A lot more than our engagements in the present day. Once a man and woman were espoused, they were already completely committed to each other. They could not even call off the wedding without a formal divorce.

Joseph had the opportunity to disgrace Mary as he probably felt she had disgraced him. If he had taken her before the priest, she probably would have been stoned to death. But because he was honorable, he honored Mary and decided to keep this situation private. Before Joseph heard from God, he displayed a godly character.

Then, the dream. Can you imagine the realization that years of prophecy are being fulfilled before your eyes and at the care of your hands? Joseph obeyed God, loved Mary, and raised God's son, Jesus, to have a godly character, too. What an awesome responsibility! What an awesome privilege!

Will you be ready to do the right thing even when adversity comes? God is looking for people who trust Him and make "just" decisions. Let God use you.

Read the story for yourself. The birth of Jesus:

Matthew 1:18–23

Luke 1:5–80; 2:1–39

What does it mean to you?

> John, the Baptist, who was now in prison, heard about all the things the Messiah was doing. So, he sent his disciples to Jesus, "Are you really the Messiah we've been waiting for, or should we keep looking for someone else?"
>
> —Matthew 11:2–3 (NLT)

Everyone, even John the Baptist, experiences moments of discouragement and "low" faith. John knew Jesus. John preferred Jesus. John sent his own disciples to become the disciples of another man: Jesus.

> Then John said, "I saw the Holy Spirit descending like a dove from heaven and resting upon him. I didn't know he was the one, but when God sent me to baptize with water, he told me, 'When you see the Holy Spirit descending and resting upon someone, he is the one you are looking for, He is the one who baptizes with the Holy Spirit.' I saw this happen to Jesus, so I testify that he is the Son of God."
>
> —John 1:32–34

John absolutely knew Jesus was God's Son. He witnessed a sign given to him by God and, therefore, boldly testified that Jesus was the Son of God. So why doubt now?

John needed reassurance. Imprisoned for doing no wrong, he called upon Jesus. The rest of the story, we know: John, never released from prison, was beheaded. He entered heaven as his own words came to pass:

> [Jesus] must increase and I must decrease.
>
> —John 3:30 (KJV)

Are you willing to be persecuted for righteousness' sake?

> Then the disciples worshiped him. "You really are the Son of God!" they exclaimed.
>
> —Matthew 14:33 (NLT)

What's it going to take for you to believe? The disciples have been with Jesus through many miracles up to this point. To name a few, He had healed a leper, a demon-possessed man, the blind, the mute, and the paralyzed, and He had fed the five thousand! But it took Jesus saving Peter from drowning for them to exclaim, "You really are the Son of God!"

I was thinking about this, and then it hit me! Peter was a disciple. Jesus walking on water and working miracles for others, although awe-inspiring, lacked personal importance for the disciples. But now, Jesus had saved one of them! This was personal.

Jesus promises us tribulation in the world, but He also promises us salvation. If you find yourself stuck in the middle of the sea with waves crashing all around you, reach out for Jesus's hand. Let Him become your personal Savior and show Himself to you as the true Son of God.

Whatever your situation today, Jesus holds the answer. Call out to Him.

What situations in your life remind you of Peter sinking in the sea during the storm?

Look back upon that situation. Can you see the hand of Jesus reaching out to you?

> Is it against the law for me to do what I want with my money? Should you be angry because I am kind?
>
> —Matthew 20:15 (NLT)

"It's just not fair!"—the cry of so many people from every generation.

The reply of others: "No one ever said life was fair."

What is fair?

Is equal fair?

Many would choose to examine equal rights of minorities, women, children, the disabled, or the elderly when discussing fair and equal. We all reached the agreement in the 1960s that "separate, but equal" was not actually equal at all. Then, there are others who do not even agree with equality at all.

> Your blood has ransomed people for God from every tribe and language and people and nation.
>
> —Revelation 5:9

In God's eyes, each individual is offered the same redemption. Jesus died for all sin, for all people, no exclusions. Each of us has an equal opportunity to be forgiven. That's equality, and that's fair.

The difference enters by way of our choices. Will you accept the offer? Will you think it unfair and reject Jesus because of your ideals and views of others?

Don't be angry when others receive the blessings of God. Rather, rejoice in your own salvation. You are an individual. Agree to serve God, no matter what! Decide today to stop comparing yourself to others. Be careful what you judge as fair and equal. Be mindful of God's just weights and balances. Rejoice, and again I say, rejoice. Salvation is yours; receive it gladly.

Read the following passages and document your thoughts.

Matthew 9:30

Matthew 20:16

Mark 10:17–31

Luke 13:22–30

> The scriptures declare, "My temple will be called a place of prayer," but you have turned it into a den of thieves!
>
> —Matthew 21:13

Remember the laws of sacrifice? A lamb without spot or blemish, perhaps two turtle doves, or a young bullock; all of these were to be the best of the flock. Depending upon your financial status or the type of atonement you were seeking, there were options so that all could come to the Lord and be cleansed for a year. However, one rule must be followed: your sacrifice was required to be perfect. The very best you could offer.

The money changers sold sacrifices for a profit. The temple would only accept one specific type of coin for the offering, and the rate of exchange was often crooked and deceitful to foreigners. People stopped searching their own flocks for the perfect sacrifice and depended upon the ease of purchasing a sacrifice at the temple door. Meeting the standard rudiment became the norm. Missing the intention behind this icon that God had set in order years before, people abandoned personal sacrifice and ritualistically attended the temple.

Jesus, knowing He was about to become the perfect, final sacrifice, passionately cleansed the temple with the hope that the worshipers might return to true worship. Jesus always uncovered sin, forcing the sinner to deal with it in repentance or else deny it and continue in sin. Jesus reminded the people of why they came to the temple: to pray. The temple should be a house of prayer.

When I think about a perfect sacrifice, oftentimes, I don't even want to put a crumpled dollar in the offering. We should always offer our best. What has the temple become for you? Why do you attend church service? Search your motives. Return to the place where you simply come to seek Jesus.

> [Jesus said,] My soul is exceeding sorrowful, even unto death: tarry ye here, and watch with me.
>
> —Matthew 26:38 (KJV)

> My soul is crushed with grief to the point of death. Stay here and watch with me.
>
> —Matthew 26:38 (NLT)

So many times, we turn the death of Jesus into a storybook tale with a happy ending: the resurrection. I truly appreciate the reality of suffering depicted by Mel Gibson's *The Passion of the Christ*. Jesus came from heaven, God's son, and lived as a man.

Jesus experienced temptation and felt pain. Emotional pain struck His heart as He was betrayed and abandoned by His closest friends. He also felt physical pain, unbearable to the point of death, yet He continued in suffering.

Verse 42 demonstrated the battle between flesh and spirit as Jesus asked of God, His Father, if there be any other way. Jesus, as a man, did not want to suffer and die. Yet, Jesus, as our Savior, was willing to fulfill the plan of the Father. Are you willing to give up your plans and your feelings in order to complete God's will in your life?

In verse 53, Jesus says,

> Don't you realize that I could ask my Father for thousands of angels to protect us, and He would send them instantly?

Jesus knew the reality of the power of God! How much more difficult for Him to continue suffering, knowing all He had to do was speak the word and angels would be summoned to deliver Him! Jesus overcame temptation. Jesus bore our punishment because of love.

This was not easy for Jesus. He did not use some supernatural anesthesia to help Him get through it. The crucifixion of Jesus, the ultimate sacrifice, a labor of love, secured redemption for all mankind. Will you accept it?

Will you believe in Jesus?

It's as easy as ABC:

A. Admit you are a sinner.

B. Believe that Jesus is God's only Son, that He died for you, that He rose again, and that He sends His spirit to dwell within you.

C. Confess your sins to God, and He is faithful and just to forgive you.

Thy will be done.

—Matthew 26:42

If you haven't heard Hillary Scott's song, "Thy Will Be Done," then go to YouTube and listen. The message of her lyrics mimics Jesus just before He goes to the cross to take away the sins of the world. He struggles with the pain and suffering He will soon experience, but nevertheless, He accepts the will of the Father.

Similarly, as circumstances of life overwhelm us, we are faced with difficult decisions and unanswerable questions. With each new tragic incident, I hear people exclaim, "Why would God allow this to happen?" I cannot answer the whys.

What I do know is that God is real. God does hear our prayers. God is just. God loves you. God loves me.

Jesus says in Matthew 5:45, "For he maketh the sun to rise on the evil and on the good, and sendeth rain on the just and on the unjust." Life happens to us all. Sometimes it's good, and sometimes it's bad. We must choose to praise God through the victories and defeats. If we concede to allow His will to be fulfilled in our lives, then we are guaranteed a resurrection-after-death experience.

It's not all rainbows and puppies serving the Lord. But the benefits are out of this world! Trust Him today.

What is an experience in which you felt like God did not answer your prayers?

Can you look back on that situation in your life and find anything good that came from it?

Can you see that God works even through the trials and tribulations of life?

> Don't be afraid. Just trust me.
>
> —Mark 5:36 (NLT)

Easy for you to say; hard for me to do. Isn't this the attitude we take when faced with uncertain situations that are out of our control? Fear creeps in, and many times, we let it take residence.

Jairus had every reason to be afraid. On his way home, with Jesus walking beside him, Jairus receives the word that his twelve-year-old daughter has already died. Her miracle was on the way, but it was not on time. Our time anyway.

If we have a problem, and we want God to remedy it, then we must give our trouble completely to God. It is not for to us to show God how or when to move. God knows the future; God knows best. Trust God.

Jesus comforted Jairus with the words, "Don't be afraid. Just trust me." No doubt Jesus could sense the fear and despair within Jairus's spirit as he received the report. Pressing past the fear, Jairus led Jesus to his home, where an even greater miracle was awaiting them.

"Just trust me." Love, Jesus.

Document a situation in your life, either past or present, where it seemed God wasn't on time—however, as you reexamine the situation, you realize that God's timing was perfect!

[Jesus] added, "It is the thought-life that defiles you. For from within, out of a person's heart, come evil thoughts, sexual immorality, theft, murder, adultery, greed, wickedness, deceit, eagerness for lustful pleasure, envy, slander, pride, and foolishness. All these vile things come from within; they are what defile you and make you unacceptable to God."

—Mark 7:20–23 (NLT)

"Unacceptable to God": this phrase is not mentioned in our King James Version. But as we live our lives, if we walk in sin, we are unacceptable to God. Unconfessed and unrepented sin is unforgivable. What is in your heart?

David prayed to the Lord in Psalm 139:23–24:

Search me, O God, and know my heart: try me, and know my thoughts: And see if there be any wicked way in me, and lead me in the way everlasting.

Open yourself up today. Let God examine your innermost feelings, emotions, and intents. He is able to renew a right spirit within you (Psalm 51).

Work as diligently on your inward self as you do your outward appearance, and you will see a glowing change. The glory of the Lord will light upon you so that others might be drawn to Jesus and seek Him for themselves, too.

When I think about ways to improve my outward features, that's easy: diet, exercise, new clothes, wash my hair, etc.

What are some ways you can improve your routine for your inward self?

One step at time.

Name one thing you will do differently starting today:

> And his disciples answered him, "From whence can a man satisfy these men with bread here in the wilderness?"
>
> —Mark 8:4

To claim to be believers, we claim to know the truth of who God is, yet still we walk in confusion and want. What's it going to take to remember who Jesus is? Jesus is not simply a man!

As I was reading this story of Jesus miraculously feeding the four thousand, I was reminded of God's provision of manna. Millions were fed for years in the wilderness by God's hand. Is it so hard to think that Jesus could multiply seven loaves to feed four thousand or more?

It seems as if the disciples were continuously amazed by Jesus's miracles. They recognized Jesus as God's son, but they still lacked understanding of His power. Jesus even asked them, "How is it that ye do not understand?" (Mark 8:21).

> And God said, "Let there be light: and there was light."
>
> —Genesis 1:2

> In the midst of the valley which was full of bones…they were very dry…I prophesied as he commanded me, and the breath came into them, and they lived, and stood up upon their feet, an exceeding great army.
>
> —Ezekiel 37:1–10

God is the creator. He creates something from nothing! We cannot figure it out because it's impossible to us, but God can just speak the word and create.

Can't you understand? Jesus is God! He is not only able, but willing!

Read the entire story from Ezekiel 37:1–10. I love the part when God asks, "Can these bones live?" and the prophet simply replies, "God, you know." God knows all, sees all, and is concerned with all.

Read Matthew 8:5–13.

Be encouraged today by the faith of the centurion. Recognizing the power of Jesus, he said, "Speak the word only." He had a faith unlike so many. I pray you have centurion faith today!

> It seemed good to me also, having had perfect understanding of all things from the very first, to write unto thee in order, most excellent Theophilus.
>
> —Luke 1:3

As a math major, I can appreciate the book of Luke. Order is very important to me. I like my things in order, my home in order, my desk in order, and to get the problem correct, my math steps must be in order, too.

Luke appreciated the records of others, as eyewitnesses, who recorded the events of Christ's life from their viewpoints. But Luke wanted to be even more thorough. He said he had "perfect understanding." He was confident in his account of Jesus's story, and we can read this historical documentation with faith.

Luke was a doctor and well educated. Luke's account of the birth, life, and death of our Lord is my favorite. As you read the Word of God, remember, you are reading truth.

Read Luke 1:1–4.

What do you learn from Luke's introduction?

> Annas and Caiaphas were the high priests. At this time a message from God came to John, son of Zechariah, who was living out in the wilderness.
>
> —Luke 3:2

You would expect a message from God to come to the high priests, but it didn't. John, at only thirty years old, was quite the wild man, not exactly preaching material. He dressed in animal skins, lived in the wilderness, and ate locusts and honey. Weird, right?

But God chose him. John heard God. John boldly proclaimed the message of repentance.

When sinners approached John, they wanted to know how to change. From soldiers to ordinary men, John told them all the same thing: give to others, make right choices, and be content with what you have. Basically, John encouraged integrity in every walk of life.

Don't make Christianity too hard. Choose Jesus, repent of your sins, and be an unselfish person of integrity. Anybody can do it. Be a modern-day John the Baptist, and don't conform to a man-made ideal, but listen for a message from God.

How have you tried to "be a Christian"?

Do you believe in Jesus?

Do you love Him with all of your heart, soul, mind, and strength?

Describe what being a Christian means to God. Really think about what God wants.

> Jesus reached out and touched the man. "I want to," he said. "Be healed."
>
> —Luke 5:13

> I am not even worthy to come and meet you. Just say the word from where you are, and my servant will be healed.
>
> —Luke 7:7

In Luke chapter 5, Jesus told the man that He wanted to heal him. In Luke chapter 7, we find the centurion having faith that believed even just a word spoken by Jesus was enough.

We serve a God who is both willing and able. Jesus came to this world with the sole purpose for us to be saved, healed, and delivered. The word for *salvation* in the Greek means all three of these things: saved, healed, and delivered. On the cross, Jesus took care of it all.

Sometimes, it seems so easy for us to repeat a simple prayer and believe God has wiped away our sin, but when it comes to a visual healing or physical deliverance, our faith crumbles. Jesus did it! Do you believe it? Jesus came to this world over two thousand years ago, God as man, lived a sinless life, died upon the cross for us, and defeated death, hell, and the grave when He rose from the dead. All of this so we can be saved, healed, and delivered. He is willing and able today. Call on Him.

Talk to Jesus today. Tell Him that you believe He is indeed willing and able to meet your needs.

> A farmer went out to plant some seed. As he scattered it across his field, some seed fell on a footpath, where it was stepped on, and the birds came and ate it. Other seed fell on shallow soil with underlying rock. This seed began to grow, but soon it withered and died for lack of moisture. Other seed fell among thorns that shot up and choked the tender blades. Still other seed fell on fertile soil. This seed grew and produced a crop one hundred times as much as had been planted.
>
> —Luke 8:4–8

Jesus often spoke in parables or stories. I've heard it said that a parable is simply an earthly story with a heavenly meaning. Oftentimes, scholars differ in their interpretations of parables. We mustn't forget the culture and people to whom Jesus spoke. In order to fully understand, we must read all of the context in which He was speaking. A reader cannot pick and choose scripture to fit his or her need. The above passage is one of my favorites because Jesus Himself gave the interpretation.

> This is the meaning of the story: The seed is God's message. The seed that fell on the hard path represents those who hear the message, but then the Devil comes and steals it away and prevents them from believing and being saved. The rocky soil represents those who hear the message with joy. But, like young plants in such soil, their roots don't go very deep. They believe for a while, but they wilt when the hot winds of testing blow. The thorny ground represents those who hear and accept the message, but all too quickly the message is crowded out by the cares and riches and pleasures of this life. And so they never grow into maturity. But the good soil represents honest, good-hearted people who hear God's message, cling to it, and steadily produce a large harvest.
>
> —Luke 8:11–15

My Bible has a subtitle for this parable: "Jesus tells the parable of the four soils." As I was reading, I misread the title as "Jesus tells the parable of the four souls." Only one letter difference in the words *soil* and *soul*, but what a difference that one letter makes! It personalizes the entire story. Your soul is that soil. It is up to you to prepare the soil for planting time and harvest. Put up a scarecrow, throw out the rocks, and pluck up the thorns. My interpretation: the scarecrow equates to Jesus on the cross. He paid the price so the devil cannot come in and steal your seed. The rocks equate to habits and poor acquaintances that weigh you down and pull you back to your past life. The thorns represent your day-to-day busy-ness, which steals your time and leaves you feeling empty and malnourished.

Jesus said, "Deny [yourself], and take up [your] cross daily, and follow me" (Luke 9:23).

It's a daily walk, just as tending a garden is a daily job. Prepare your soul as a farmer prepares his soil, and you too will reap a bountiful harvest.

What condition is your soil in? Your soul?

> "But you," He asked them, "who do you say that I am?"
>
> —Luke 9:20

Many rumors were being spread about Jesus. As He went from town to town, He healed, saved, and delivered. Many signs followed Him. He fed five thousand men, plus women and children, with only five loaves of bread and two fish, and His disciples gathered up twelve baskets of leftovers. Yes! Jesus was quite famous.

And much like famous people today, He had followers and critics. People speculated who He really could be and perform such miracles. Could He be a prophet of old reincarnate? Was He John the Baptist resurrected? Confusion everywhere.

People are still confused today. Many are led astray by mysticism, new religions, and false prophets. Society does not want to recognize the deity of Christ. But there is no other. Jesus is the son of God. Jesus is the only way.

> Jesus told him, "I am the way, the truth, and the life. No one comes to the Father except through me."
>
> —John 14:6

The disciples answered Jesus, "You are the Son of God."

Who do you say that Jesus is?

> Rejoice with me, because I have found my lost sheep!
>
> —Luke 15:6b

This entire chapter is one of my favorites: the lost sheep, the lost coin, and the prodigal son. In the New Living Translation, verses 7 and 10 begin with "In the same way there is joy." We can relate to the joy we might feel when we have found an item of great value that was lost. How inspiring to know that "In the same way there is joy" in heaven and among the angels when a lost person finds the Lord!

Verse 20 tugs on my heartstrings, too. "So [the son] returned home to his father. And while he was still a long way off, his father saw him coming. Filled with love and compassion, he ran to his son, embraced him, and kissed him." I like to imagine "in the same way" our Heavenly Father seeing us from afar off and, being filled with love and compassion toward us, running to meet us. I believe He runs to embrace us with open, loving arms, restoring the relationship we broke due to our sin.

Then there is the older brother. Verses 28–32 tell an all-too-familiar story of selfishness and unforgiveness.

The "good" son, as some might call him, returns home from working in the fields. He hears the party, inquires about the hoopla, and then becomes angry because he never had a party and he does not believe his brother deserves a party. I trust we can learn from this, as well. The verse for today exclaims, "Rejoice with me!" I hope we can find it in ourselves to rejoice with others when they choose Jesus! Don't judge people by their actions when they were lost, but rather, rejoice that they have been found.

Our Heavenly Father threw a party in heaven the day we called upon Him. With love and compassion, He embraced us even in our filth. Now we must embrace and celebrate others.

Have you judged others too harshly?

Who might you need to have compassion upon today?

Remember, if God embraces you in your sin, how much more should we embrace others.

> Jesus replied, "If you only knew the gift God has for you and who you are speaking to, you would ask me, and I would give you living water."
>
> —John 4:9b

We moved to the country when I was eight years old. So many of my childhood memories are from country living, and the majority of my dreams occur in the setting of our country home. Living just around the corner from Grannie and Papa, I spent many days and nights at my grandparents' house. Memories: the chickens, the cows, the garden, the early mornings, the embarrassing pink asbestos siding, the coconut cake, the dishwashing liquid bubble baths, the popcorn and glass bottle of Dr. Pepper, the half piece of gum, and so much more.

One of my most unique memories from Grannie's house revolves around the water bucket. Sitting to the right of the kitchen sink, up on the counter, rested an old enamel pot and ladle, white with red trim. Each morning, Grannie would fill the pot with fresh water—perhaps from the well, I really don't know.

All throughout the day, we would work and play, and whenever we needed a drink of water, to the pot we would go. Grab the ladle, scoop up some water, and drink away. Mmmmmm....refreshing. No worries or concerns for germs. We all drank from the same ladle and same bucket. At my house, we had no pot or ladle. At my house, we had to use a cup! But at Grannie's house, I loved to drink from the ladle.

Jesus does not want you to settle for drinking out of a boring old cup. He offers living water!

I love this passage of scripture: "Jesus says, 'If you only knew.'" Praise God, I know! Jesus is God's Son, and He holds the bucket. Let Him saturate you. All you need to do is ask.

Turn on a praise song today. Sit in the presence of God. Feel His Spirit wash over you. Do you feel refreshed? Alive?

> Then he stooped down again and wrote in the dust.
>
> —John 8:8

Man, I want more information! What did Jesus write? Could He have listed each man's sins? Perhaps He just drew a picture? Maybe He just wanted an excuse to kneel at eye level with the accused? That last thought sounds like Jesus to me.

This woman not only was accused of committing adultery, but she was "caught in the very act." In my mind, I can only imagine she was set up as a way to try to test Jesus and His knowledge of the law. The men proclaimed that Moses commanded that she must be stoned to death.

Where was the man? If this woman, thrown to the ground as a spectacle for all to see, was caught in the very act, then where was the man? For the law of Moses actually commanded that both of them should be stoned to death (Deuteronomy 22).

Jesus stooped and wrote on the ground. I'm thinking the woman could sense His presence close to her as He brought Himself to her level. What did He write? Oh, how I want to know!

We just don't have a record of what Jesus wrote on the ground or why, but thankfully, we know what He said to this woman, clearly a sinner: "Let the one who has never sinned throw the first stone!" (verse 7, NLT). One by one, the accusers dropped their stones and walked away. Jesus told the woman that He did not condemn her, and that she should "Go and sin no more" (verse 11).

We are not called to judge others but to show them the love and mercy of Christ. Does that mean we condone the sin? Absolutely not. Jesus forgives but instructs us to go and sin no more. Continue living, but stop sinning. Live your life differently now that you've encountered the Lord.

There are many questions for which I do not have the answers, but I choose to focus on the truth I know: Jesus loves me; Jesus forgives me; now I must daily go and sin no more.

Are you living in sin?

Jesus loves you, and He will forgive you. Ask Him.

Now continue living, but stop sinning.

Jesus answered, "I tell you the truth."

—John 8:58

Beginning in verse 12 and continuing through verse 59, Jesus refers to truth twelve times. If 1 Corinthians 13 is the love chapter, then surely John 8 can be called the truth chapter. Verse 44 proclaims, "[The devil] has always hated the truth, because there is no truth in him. When he lies it is consistent with his character; for he is a liar and the father of lies."

So many people have heard the lies of the devil and believed them to be truth. We must use caution when reading the news, social media, and the like, so that we distinguish truth from lies. Embellishments and hearsay have a way of misinterpreting truth. Do you remember the game we played as children called telephone? Children line up, and the first whispers a message to the next, who whispers to the next, and so on until the final person reveals the message aloud. Usually, the message changes considerably from the start.

The only way to reveal truth is to hear it from the source. John 8:58: "Jesus, answered, 'I tell you the truth, before Abraham was even born, I AM.'" Jesus tells the truth because He is the source.

Take time to read John 8 today. What truth do you find in the words of Jesus?

> "Why was this man born blind? Was it because of his own sins or his parent's sins?"
>
> "It was not because of his sins or his parent's sins," Jesus answered.
>
> —John 9:2

We cannot explain away the world's problems so easily. Oh my, how I've tried! I am guilty of thoughts such as these: "If only I hadn't _____, then my children wouldn't have suffered _____." (Fill in the blanks multiple times over.)

I have witnessed other people suffering in the hospital after heart attack, stroke, or infection. Many times, people ask, "What did I do to deserve this?"

It's especially difficult when we are faced with the death of a loved one. The heartache seems unbearable at times. Those of us who are left behind ask, "Why would God allow this person to die?"

So many questions, all with the same unfulfilling answer: "I don't know."

But one thing I do know: God is still God. He loves me. And if, during these dark, lonely, confusing moments, I would run into His arms instead of blaming Him, I would find love, healing, and unexplainable joy.

Easy, right?

Absolutely not!

It is a daily battle. A battle against despair. A battle against the "norm." Daily we battle with confidence that Jesus has already won the war.

> These things I have spoken unto you, that in me ye might have peace. In the world ye shall have tribulation: but be of good cheer; I have overcome the world.
>
> —John 16:33

Do you have any questions for God? Don't be afraid to ask Him. He knows your thoughts anyway, so just be honest and sincere as you pray. In the Psalms, King David once said, "I water my couch with my tears" (Psalm 6:6). You will not shock God or hurt His feelings.

Be honest with Him today, and He will wrap His loving arms of comfort around you and grant you peace even in the unknown.

> Jesus also did many other things. If they were all written down, I suppose the whole world could not contain the books that would be written.
>
> —John 21:25 (NLT)

Can you imagine? There are so many unanswered questions and so much I want to know about Jesus's life. The disciples recorded a few snippets of His life, but writing was not as accessible two thousand years ago. I am grateful for the words we have.

One reason I am writing this book is to encourage you to read for yourself. The stories we do have document the love, grace, and mercy Jesus offers.

The Bible is no ordinary book but has withstood the test of time. Scrolls were protected and hidden so the Words of Life would be preserved for future generations. Copies were hand-crafted by men dedicated to God. Authenticity of the gospel has been provided by eyewitness accounts of the life and miracles of Jesus.

Even the Jews and Muslims regard Jesus as a prophet. His works and existence cannot be refuted. Sadly, they still seek another Messiah. As Christians, we must strive to show Jesus to others through our daily lives and everyday actions. Live a life of love.

Do you have a favorite Bible story about Jesus? Share it here on this page and find someone to share it with today.

> Then they put their hands over their ears and began shouting.
>
> —Acts 7:57 (NLT)

The story of Stephen has always been one of my favorites. Beginning with Acts 6:5, we meet "Stephen, a man full of faith and the Holy Ghost" (KJV). Stephen had been going about preaching the good news of Jesus and performing miracles. This brought him to the attention of the temple rulers. Men began to debate with Stephen; but none could match Stephen's wisdom, so they decided to spread rumors against him. Stephen was arrested.

As he was brought before the council and questioned, Stephen boldly responded. I find Stephen's response compelling (Acts 7:2–53). The Bible says Stephen's face shone like an angel (Acts 6:15). Stephen began with a history story upon which everyone could agree. He started his defense with the story of Moses. He reminded the leaders of Moses receiving the law on Mount Sinai, a law which they all upheld and believed. However, Stephen also reminded them of the shamefulness in their history: "But our ancestors refused to listen to Moses. They rejected him and wanted to return to Egypt" (verse 39). They all stood by and intently listened to all Stephen had to say, even agreeing with his every word. Until verse 51, when Stephen said, "Must you forever resist the Holy Spirit? That's what your ancestors did, and so do you!" Stephen called them murderers of Jesus, the Messiah.

Have you ever talked with children, and when they didn't like what you had to say, they put their hands over their ears? Perhaps once you were that child! It's high time we listen! Sometimes the truth hurts. We can be quick to judge others and understand the judgment of those in the history books. As onlookers, we see the foolishness and arrogance that leads to destruction. But looking in the mirror oftentimes puts us on the defensive. We do not want to see our mistakes, admit wrongdoing, or change.

These leaders of the temple could not stand to hear Stephen's accusations because they were guilty. The King James Version says they "gnashed" on him with their teeth (verse 54). Can you imagine grown men biting another grown man? They were chaotic in their charge against the righteous man, Stephen. As they stoned him to death, he had a vision of Jesus and forgave them as he died (verses 56–59).

Do you find yourself just going through the motions of Christianity? Do you find yourself quick to judge others and hanging on every line of the law simply to accuse them of failure?

Find a relationship with Jesus today. Certainly He wants you to serve Him, but He wants you to serve from a heart of love. Spread the good news to others in such a fashion that they will actually believe that Jesus is good!

> Who are you, Lord?
>
> —Acts 9:5

Stephen's life, though cut short, impacted many for the future of the gospel. Consider the bystander, Saul.

> His accusers took off their coats and laid them at the feet of a young man named Saul.
>
> —Acts 7:58

> Saul was one of the witnesses, and he agreed completely with the killing of Stephen.
>
> —Acts 8:1

> Meanwhile, Saul was uttering threats with every breath and was eager to kill the Lord's followers.
>
> —Acts 9:1

Saul was a zealot. He felt justified and righteous in the act of condemning and killing the Christians. A Jew by birth, Saul was taught the ways of his faith and law at the feet of Gamaliel, a great and famous Jewish leader of the time. He witnessed the death of Stephen, did nothing to stop it, and was even compliant. I can only imagine that hearing Stephen pray, "Lord, don't charge them with this sin!" (7:59) plagued Saul in the night.

Stephen's exhortation lined up so perfectly with all Saul had been taught as a Jewish boy except for the part about Jesus. How could a man condemned to die forgive his accusers amidst such torture? These thoughts possibly haunted Saul as he persecuted others for practicing this new faith.

Saul believed in God. Saul followed the law. Saul sought to defend his God, his faith, at any cost. The same zeal made Saul, as convert Paul, a mighty Christian.

Saul thought he knew the Lord, but on his way to persecute Christians in Damascus, Saul encountered the Lord for real. Acts 9:3–5 describes this encounter:

> A light from heaven suddenly shone down around him. He fell to the ground and heard a voice saying to him, "Saul, Saul! Why are you persecuting me?"
>
> "Who are you, Lord?" Saul replied.
>
> And the voice replied, "I am Jesus, the one you are persecuting!"

Wow! I love Saul's question: "Who are you, Lord?" Saul had thought he was serving God all along, but his faith had been based on actions and not relationship. He had lost sight of who God was, and therefore, Saul could not recognize the deity of Jesus. In persecuting Christians, Saul indeed persecuted Christ. Saul encountered Jesus, and it changed everything!

Seek a relationship with the Lord, allow Him to show you who He is, and accept Jesus as your Lord today. He changes everything!

Do you remember when you first discovered Jesus?

Record your "Damascus story":

> But while Peter was in prison, the church prayed very earnestly for him.
>
> —Acts 12:5 (NLT)

There are many different kinds of prisons in this life. There is the actual, physical building with cells and bars where many people are contained. There is a prison of your mind, where your thoughts control you, and therefore, you feel trapped rather than free. If you ask teenagers, they might proclaim school is their prison because it's a requirement they cannot change. Some people suffer in a prison of circumstance and feel backed into a corner with no chance of escape.

Fear not, because God still works miracles. "The Lord has sent His angel and saved me" (Acts 12:11b). Peter thought he was experiencing a vision, but the reality was that God heard the prayers of His people and sent an angel to perform a mighty work, an unexplainable work, a supernatural work. Prayer changes things.

I encourage you today to join your faith with that of others and pray together. Philippians 4:6 declares, "Don't worry about anything; instead, pray about everything. Tell God what you need, and thank him for all he has done" (NLT). I believe that just as God moved on behalf of Peter, God will send His angel to the secret places and supernaturally, unexplainably, and mightily move on your behalf, too!

What circumstances have you feeling imprisoned?

Be free today! The Lord has sent His angel to save you.

The Roman Road (NLT)

> No one is righteous—not even one.
>
> —Romans 3:10
>
> For everyone has sinned; we all fall short of God's glorious standard.
>
> —Romans 3:23
>
> But God showed His great love for us by sending Christ to die for us while we were still sinners.
>
> —Romans 5:8
>
> For the wages of sin is death, but the free gift of God is eternal life through Christ Jesus our Lord.
>
> —Romans 6:23
>
> So now there is no condemnation for those who belong to Christ Jesus.
>
> —Romans 8:1
>
> If you openly declare that Jesus is Lord and believe in your heart that God raised him from the dead, you will be saved.
>
> —Romans 10:9

When I was growing up in the Baptist church, these scriptures represented the approachability of God through Jesus. We all fall into the same category: sinner. I am no better than you. You are no better than me. But for the grace of God, we would all be condemned. We can all be freed from the wages and condemnation of our sin because of Jesus.

Memorize the verses from the Roman Road. If you learn one a day, you will know them all in a week's time!

Meditate upon each verse. What does it mean for you and your life? How can you share these promises with others?

The book of Romans offers encouragement and direction for us in our walk with Christ. I encourage you to take time to read the entire book today. It's only sixteen chapters. Over the next few days, I'm simply going to list a few of my favorite scriptures. Ponder them in your heart. Journal what they speak to you.

> And we know that all things work together for good to them that love God, to them who are the called according to his purpose.
>
> —Romans 8:28

I quote this one all the time! What joy and reassurance can you find in these precious words?

> What shall we then say to these things? If God be for us, who can be against us? ... Who shall separate us from the love of Christ? Shall tribulation, or distress, or persecution, or famine, or nakedness, or peril, or sword? As it is written, For thy sake we are killed all the day long; we are accounted as sheep for the slaughter. Nay, in all these things we are more than conquerors through him that loved us. For I am persuaded, that neither death, nor life, nor angels, nor principalities, nor powers, nor things present, nor things to come, nor height, nor depth, nor any other creature, shall be able to separate us from the love of God, which is in Christ Jesus our Lord.
>
> —Romans 8:31, 35–39

Yes! Yes! Yes! I am more than a conqueror! God loves me, and no one or nothing can change that fact!

How does this make you feel today?

> For whosoever shall call upon the name of the Lord shall be saved.
>
> —Romans 10:13

I am a whosoever! You are a whosoever! Whom can you share this good news with today?

> I beseech you therefore, brethren, by the mercies of God, that ye present your bodies a living sacrifice, holy, acceptable unto God, which is your reasonable service. And be not conformed to this world: but be ye transformed by the renewing of your mind, that ye may prove what is that good, and acceptable, and perfect, will of God.
>
> —Romans 12:1–2

Wow! What does "reasonable service" mean to you?

As you reflect upon your life, do you see ways you have conformed to the world? How can you be different?

How can you renew your mind? (If you get stuck here, read Philippians 4:8.)

First Corinthians 13:1–13.

Grab a Bible. Please read the entire chapter.

I love "love." I am the romantic. My choice will be romance over thriller, action, sci-fi, etc., every time! As we travel, I look for souvenirs that say *love* in any language or form. It's my thing, my calling card; it makes me smile. Love.

So, I must include the "love" chapter of the Bible in our journal. What exactly is love? How should the action verb *love* look? All you need to know can be found in 1 Corinthians 13.

Without love, I would be nothing (verse 2).

Without love, my works are worthless (verse 3).

When I practice patience, kindness, and humility, that is love (verse 4).

When I prefer others, give of myself, control my attitude, and forgive others, that is love (verse 5).

When I tell the truth and stand up for truth, that is love (verse 6).

When I fall but try again; when I continue living even in pain; when I expect the best even when I see the worst, that is love (verse 7).

Even when all else crumbles, love remains (verse 8).

I don't understand my circumstances, but as a child of God, I endure knowing God's got me (verses 9–12).

You just can't beat love (verse 13).

Reread 1 Corinthians 13 today. Jot down a few examples of love evident in your day-to-day life.

> As though I had been born at the wrong time, I also saw him.
>
> —1 Corinthians 15:8

The apostle Paul never met Jesus face to face when Jesus was alive on the earth during His three and a half years of ministry. Jesus's life was witnessed by many, beginning with the group of shepherds who visited Him as a babe in a manger and climaxing with as many as five thousand men plus women and children whom Jesus fed and ministered unto. Many, many people saw or experienced firsthand the miracle-working power and loving presence of Jesus, God's son, upon the earth, but not the apostle Paul, who would have then been known as Saul.

However, after Jesus was crucified, He rose from the dead and presented Himself to many: Mary Magdalene, the eleven disciples, the two on the road to Emmaeus, and the five hundred who stood amazed as Jesus ascended into the heavens, but not the apostle Paul, still called Saul.

Before conversion, Saul went about persecuting any who declared the name of Jesus. Saul even stood by and held the coats of the men who murdered Stephen by stoning him. Saul watched Stephen proclaim, "I see [Jesus] standing on the right hand of God" (Acts 7:55). As Stephen looked up into the heavens and saw Jesus, Saul, not yet Paul, did not see Him.

Thank the Lord, for He is good, and His mercy endures forever (Psalm 106). Finally, as Saul made his way to Damascus to bring charges against the Christians, he saw Jesus. Jesus appeared to Saul along the way, spoke to him, and changed his path forever. Saul took on a new character and a new name, Paul. Paul retells the life-altering encounter every opportunity he can. I especially love this particular phrase found in 1 Corinthians 15: "As though I had been born at the wrong time, I also saw Him."

Paul may not have had the opportunity to walk with Jesus like the disciples. Paul was not there among the shepherds who found Jesus as a baby. Paul did not experience the fanfare of the wise men. Paul was not even present to witness Jesus crucified. None of that matters because Paul had a personal experience with Jesus in his own time, and that experience reshaped Paul's future.

You, too, can experience Jesus for yourself. It is His desire to dwell with you on a daily basis. You can see Him in the nature around you. You can see Him through the pages of His Word. You can see Him in the eyes of a loved one. You can see Him in the generosity and kindnesses of His family. And sometimes, when He deems it necessary, Jesus reveals Himself to people in dreams, in person, or in Spirit.

I encourage you to look for Jesus today.

Go to YouTube and listen to "You Are Holy, Oh So Holy" by Christ for the Nations.

It's one of my favorite worship songs.

> Our lives are a Christlike fragrance rising up to God. But this fragrance is perceived differently by those who are being saved and by those who are perishing. To those who are perishing, we are a dreadful smell of death and doom. But to those who are being saved, we are a life-giving perfume.
>
> —2 Corinthians 2:15–16 (NLT)

"Oooooo, po' cat!" I have never forgotten that phrase. Driving down country roads with your car windows down, you are certain to encounter skunk smell. A threatened skunk has either sprayed an enemy or met his misfortune traveling the same country road and become what's lovingly known as roadkill. My dear friend, Amy Drake, never called a skunk by its name but used the phrase "po' cat" instead. I suppose that's short for "poor cat," since the cute, but smelly, critter favors our common house cat. Skunk smell is difficult to shake. There are numerous home remedies, such as bathing in tomato juice. Fortunately, I avoided being sprayed while growing up in the country.

Now, my grandfather, Papa, had a different opinion from most. He actually liked the smell of the skunk spray! He often said he wished they could bottle skunk scent for perfume. I'm thankful I did *not* inherit Papa's sense of smell. I much prefer mint, cinnamon, spice, and everything nice.

But that's my point, isn't it? What's nice for one isn't necessarily nice for another. During the fall season, I love the smell of pumpkin. My friend, however, can't stand pumpkin, but she chooses apple pie for a favorite scent. Another friend of mine adores a rose-scented candle, but that's not a favorite of mine.

Similarly, our walks with the Lord are not all the same. Sinners, ones who don't know Christ, may be offended and wrinkle up their noses when you present your faith. Condemnation and ignorance play a huge part in their resistance. That is why it's so important for us as Christians to temper our walk with love. We want our fragrance to draw others to Jesus, not repel them like Raid! Live a godly life, be a good example, and hopefully you will attract others who are seeking with your irresistible fragrance.

Full disclosure:

After I wrote this excerpt and shared it, my mom alerted me to the fact that the term is actually *polecat*. Not *po' cat*, short for poor cat! Who knew? Apparently, everybody but me. Nevertheless, I kept my story as is because my whole life, that's what I actually believed. LOL!

Google it, and you will find that a polecat isn't a skunk at all, but its very own category of animal. However, skunks also go by that term. Interesting!

Do you stink? Spend time in the presence of the Lord today. Your prayers are a sweet-smelling savor to Him. When you leave his presence, you will "smell" better to others, too.

> For we live by believing and not by seeing.
>
> —2 Corinthians 5:7

In the meantime…

Oh, Lord, how I want my eyes to be opened to You. I want to see others how You see them. I want to see myself how You see me. I want to know Your perfect plans. I want to see through eyes of unconditional love, eyes of grace, and eyes of compassion.

Wouldn't that be wonderful?

Unfortunately, most of the time, I just can't "see" it. God's perfect plan for my life is not rolled out before me like a treasure map. Life often seems more like a maze than a map. I have run slap-dab into a dead end and had to retrace my steps to find another route. Sometimes, I feel as if I'm wandering in circles. Other times, my way gets shrouded in darkness, and I grope to make my way out. What then?

Reading this scripture was like a slap in the face. "Wake up, Amy! You don't have to see to live; just trust Me." Wow!

Isn't that what Christianity is all about? Being a believer. Believing God works on my behalf, even when I cannot see the results.

> Faith shows the reality of what we hope for; it is the evidence of things we cannot see.
>
> —Hebrews 11:1 (NLT)

> And it is impossible to please God without faith. Anyone who wants to come to him must believe that God exists and that he rewards those who sincerely seek him.
>
> —Hebrews 11:6 (NLT)

Can you believe it? This common scripture conveys so much! We must believe. "We live by believing and not by seeing" (2 Corinthians 5:7). Lord, forgive me for not living my life by faith.

Contemplate yesterday's scriptures. What has God promised you? What does God's Word say about you? Do you believe Him?

The story in 2 Kings 6:8-23 is a powerful story of walking by faith and not by sight.

Read it today.

Elisha didn't see the armies of God surrounding him, yet he believed they were there. Do we want to be like the servant whose eyes were opened, or do we want to be like the prophet who believed by faith?

The story of the servant is a blessing and a wonderful story of the spiritual realm surrounding us, but upon further reflection, I desire to walk in faith, whether I see or not.

> Against such there is no law.
>
> —Galatians 5:23b

When a thing is so great! I mean, there really just aren't any negative words to be said about this thing. This thing is desired. It isn't just tolerated. It's coveted. Yet, freely given! This thing is so amazing there are no laws against it! What is it?

It isn't actually a singular thing at all, but rather a collection of character traits. The Bible calls them fruits, and you can possess them all. Let these fruits shine forth through your character in your life: love, joy, peace, longsuffering, gentleness, goodness, faith, meekness, and temperance.

Can you imagine if we all exhibited more of these fruits in our lives?

Bear the fruits, plant the seeds, and reap a harvest for a future overflowing with more love, more joy, more peace, more longsuffering, more gentleness, more goodness, more faith, more meekness, and more temperance.

How can you bear more fruit in your everyday life?

Love

Joy

Peace

Longsuffering

Gentleness

Goodness

Faith

Meekness

Temperance

> Therefore, I, a prisoner for serving the Lord, beg you to lead a life worthy of your calling, for you have been called by God. Always be humble and gentle. Be patient with each other, making allowance for each other's faults because of your love. Make every effort to keep yourselves united in the Spirit, binding yourselves together with peace.
>
> —Ephesians 4:1–3

Wow! Here writes Paul, imprisoned for preaching Jesus, and presenting you with the simplicity of how to live a Christian life. First of all, Paul assures you that you have been called! Each and every person is called to work for the Lord and to be His child.

> For God so loved the world [the entire world] that He gave His only begotten son, so that whosoever [that means you] believeth in Him should not perish by have everlasting life.
>
> —John 3:16

Certainly, you cannot be perfect, but you can strive to make better decisions. The calling is irrevocable, so you should do what you are able to do to be worthy of the calling.

What on earth does it mean to be worthy?

Paul lays out some guidelines in the following verses: be humble and gentle. These two admirable qualities may seem understated, but it takes a great man or woman to demonstrate a character of humility and gentleness.

How can you incorporate more humility and gentleness into your everyday life?

Next, Paul commands you to be patient with each other.

Patience.

Very few have mastered that craft. In this fast-food, fast-internet, and faster-speed-limit life, patience is often intolerable. Instead of demanding, "Now, now, now!", you must wait on the voice of the Lord, wait on others, and wait on your own progress, as well. Remember, you must crawl before you walk.

Paul requests that in your patience, you offer mercy and forgiveness toward others. "Making allowance for each other's faults."

Think about that quote a minute. This one hits me between the eyes!

You are not perfect, nor is anyone else. Fortunately, Paul gives us further instruction:

"Because of your love." Go back and read the entry on 1 Corinthians 13. If you act in love, you will show patience and mercy.

Finally, you receive the exhortation for unity.

"Make every effort," Paul says. It takes effort. This is not an easy path; however, the rewards are glorious. Come together peacefully.

> If it be possible, as much as lieth in you, live peaceably with all men.
>
> —Romans 12:18

I love that Paul includes "if it be possible." This a daily walk. Some people simply do not allow us to be unified with them. In this case, shake off your feet and pray for them, knowing you did your part acting in humility, gentleness, patience, and effort.

> But we are citizens of heaven.
>
> —Philippians 3:20a (NLT)

Philippians is a short letter written by Paul to his friends in Philippi. Paul has been imprisoned for preaching the good news of Jesus, but his concern is not for himself but to encourage others who might suffer a similar fate.

This simple phrase, "but we are citizens of heaven," pricked my heart. What does it mean to be a citizen? I imagine all the blessings I receive as a citizen of the United States of America. I am covered by the constitution and laws of the land. I am granted freedom of speech, the right to vote, the right to bear arms, freedom of worship, and so much more, simply because I am a citizen of the USA. When I travel to other countries, I don't travel in fear because I have the support of the American government and armed forces because I am a citizen. When I return to the USA from travels, I do not worry about crossing the border because I am a citizen. Being a citizen grants me special privileges.

How much more are the privileges of being a citizen of heaven? I am able to come boldly to the throne of grace and receive mercy because I am a citizen (Hebrews 4:16). I receive the gift of eternal life because I am a citizen (Romans 6:23, John 3:16). The angels rejoice over me because I am a citizen (Luke 15:10). Whatever I ask the Father, He hears, and He will give it to me because I am a citizen (John 16:23). The list is endless.

The best part is that becoming a citizen of heaven is free; there's no test, only one requirement: receive Jesus Christ as your Lord and Savior.

> For ye are all the children of God by faith in Christ Jesus.
>
> —Galatians 3:26 (KJV)

> But after that the kindness and love of God our Savior toward man appeared, not by works of righteousness which we have done, but according to his mercy he saved us, by the washing of regeneration, and renewing of the Holy Ghost; which he shed on us abundantly through

Jesus Christ our Savior; that being justified by his grace, we should be made heirs according to the hope of eternal life.

—Titus 3:4–7 (KJV)

Take time to read the entire book of Philippians today. It is only four chapters.

Jot down any favorite references you read.

Over the next few days, let's ponder some of my favorites.

> Being confident of this very thing, that he which hath begun a good work in you will perform it until the day of Jesus Christ.
>
> —Philippians 1:6

Are you waiting for God to complete something in you?

Think back upon your life. List some things that God has already brought to fruition. Be encouraged today.

> For unto you it is given in the behalf of Christ, not only to believe on him, but also to suffer for his sake.
>
> —Philippians 1:29

Yuck! Why this scripture? Suffering is part of the package. Unfortunately, living for Jesus is not all roses and puppies. Roses have thorns, and puppies chew up your new patio furniture (but that's a different story).

Can you think of a time when you suffered for the cause of Christ?

> Let nothing be done through strife or vainglory; but in lowliness of mind let each esteem other better than themselves. Look not every man on his own things, but every man also on the things of others. Let this mind be in you, which was also in Christ Jesus....Do all things without murmurings and disputings: That ye may be blameless and harmless, the sons of God, without rebuke, in the midst of a crooked and perverse nation, among whom ye shine as lights in the world; Holding forth the word of life; that I may rejoice in the day of Christ.
>
> —Philippians 2:3–5, 14–16a

Consider others before yourself.

Live without complaint.

Be a light.

Represent Christ.

What does this scripture mean to you?

But what things were gain to me, those I counted loss for Christ.

—Philippians 3:7

When it comes right down to it, do you choose Christ first? This is a toughie!

I can do all things through Christ which strengtheneth me.

—Philippians 4:13

You can do it!

Memorize this scripture.

All things.

All things.

All things.

> And whatsoever ye do in word or deed, do all in the name of the Lord Jesus, giving thanks to God and the Father by him.
>
> —Colossians 3:17

What constitutes working for the Lord? Is it just standing in the pulpit on a Sunday morning delivering a message to a congregation? Who fulfills the work of the Lord? Is it only pastors and teachers or those on the church payroll?

If the world depends solely on the efforts of the ministers in full-time positions of ministry, then millions of people will remain unchanged and unmoved. Ministry and outreach to others require action on the part of all believers.

The work of the Lord can take on many descriptors. Certainly, for the pastor, this does look like the traditional Sunday morning message. But it's also demonstrated by the Monday morning repair of a loose wheel, or the Friday decorating for a Valentine's banquet, or the day-to-day management of the church office. The work of the Lord takes on many forms throughout each new day.

For some, the work is accomplished as a volunteer. Little glory is received as men and women take the time out of the daily routine to pick up groceries or move tables to prepare for an upcoming food service. Tearing down tables and chairs from one occasion in order to set up others for the next even seems a daunting task, but generous-hearted people accomplish it with a smile.

The work of the Lord does not need to be extraordinary or overly difficult. This work can be performed by all on a daily basis. This work can be accomplished by multitasking. I can perform the work of the Lord. You can perform the work of the Lord, too.

Wherever you are today, as you fulfill your daily "to do" list, maintain a pleasant disposition, show kindness to others, lend a helping hand when possible, and live your life with a smile. You will bring joy to those who work alongside you. You will be an example of Jesus's love for others. And you will accomplish the work of the Lord every single day.

Colossians is another one of the short books of the Bible. Written by Paul to the church in Colosse, it's full of a wealth of good Christian advice. Take time to read the four chapters today. Document below the verses that speak the most to you.

> So encourage each other with these words.
>
> —1 Thessalonians 4:18 (NLT)

Be encouraged today and every day. God's promises are faithful and true. He never leaves us or forsakes us. Does that mean life is wonderful all the time with no troubles? Absolutely not. As a matter of fact, God tells us we indeed will have trouble. However, in our sorrow, we don't sorrow as others who have no hope (1 Thessalonians 4:13). We have hope, people!

> For since we believe that Jesus died and was raised to life again, we also believe that when Jesus returns, God will bring back with him the believers who have died.
>
> —1 Thessalonians 4:14

> The armies of heaven, dressed in the finest of pure white linen, followed him on white horses.
>
> —Revelation 19:14

This is not the end. Once you know Jesus, you begin to live, and you will continue to live an eternity with God. There is so much more to come! Be encouraged today. Encourage someone else today. Invite everyone to know Jesus and give them the opportunity of hope.

Make a list of people that you encounter on a weekly basis. To whom can you be an encouragement? How?

> In every thing give thanks: for this is the will of God in Christ Jesus concerning you.
>
> —1 Thessalonians 5:18

Waah, waaah, waaaah! Let's all just sit down and have a pity party, why don't we? Because we are bored. We have all been guilty of using this two-word phrase: "I'm bored!" I intend to show you the error of your phrase.

My mother-in-law passed away several years ago, yet she remains very much a part of our daily lives. The paint and carpet may change, but her memory lingers, still. Often her words of wisdom and godly advice flood my memory. I remember her response to the phrase, "I'm bored." I heard her many times speak these words to children and grandchildren.

"If you are bored, then you are ungrateful. God has given you so many blessings. Now go play, and be thankful for what you have."

I never would have thought that boredom could be a synonym for ungratefulness, but it makes such sense to me. I tell you the truth, if I even have the thought of being bored, now, I mentally correct myself and find something with which to busy myself.

Lord, forgive me when I'm not thankful.

I am thankful for my Christian heritage from childhood until now. The people God places in my life are a source of learning and encouragement. I give thanks to the Lord for all of my family. I give thanks to the Lord for salvation through Jesus and His unwavering love toward me. I thank God for redemption when I fail. When I call, He is faithful to hear me, and that amazes me. I'm thankful I can pass on what I have been taught to future generations. I'm thankful God would choose to use me.

Eliminate boredom with a heart filled with gratitude.

Comprise a list of things you are thankful for:

> Be not weary in well doing.
>
> —2 Thessalonians 3:13 (KJV)
>
> Never get tired of doing good.
>
> —2 Thessalonians 3:13 (NLT)

It's easy to get tired of what we are doing, even when we are doing a good thing. In Bob Sorge's book *Reset*, he says, "Refuse a cynical spirit" (p. 49). Oftentimes, we self-reflect and become convinced that we are the only ones working.

Elijah demonstrated this multiple times. He overthrew 450 prophets of Baal, spoke the word of the Lord, and performed many miraculous feats, yet, he felt weary. "I, even I only, am left; and they seek my life, to take it away" (1 Kings 19:14).

The Lord responded to Elijah's pity party saying, "Go, return on thy way" (1 Kings 19:15). Keep doing what you are doing! Don't give up yet. And, by the way, "I have left me seven thousand in Israel, all the knees which have not bowed unto Baal" (1 Kings 19:18).

You are not alone. We are not alone. The Lord remains faithful. He sees us. If we will keep doing good, and faint not, He will send us others to come alongside us. As a matter of fact, in the very next verse, Elijah found Elisha, who would walk with him, learn from him, and carry on "doing good" after Elijah was gone.

Don't give up. Do good.

What things weary you?

Call a friend. Work together. Continue doing good. Wait upon the Lord. Find renewed strength.

> The purpose of my instruction is that all believers would be filled with love that comes from a pure heart, a clear conscience, and genuine faith.
>
> —1 Timothy 1:5

Paul writes to his young protégé, Timothy, and he has a specific purpose in mind. Paul's writings are not intended to be a list of dos and don'ts for believers. Oftentimes, I tend to look at it that way. It's easy to become overwhelmed and feel defeated as we "work" to please God.

Thankfully, that's not the intention at all. Besides, Paul even tells us in 1 Timothy 1:15 that he is the worst sinner of all. Jesus uses Paul as our example, so we can know there is hope for us. "[Jesus has] great patience with even the worst of sinners" (NLT).

Paul's intention is for everyone to be filled with love. *Love.* Personally, I love "love"! (I've told you that before.) When we view life through the eyes of love, our perspective is renewed. And Paul's not referring to an "I love pizza" kind of love, but he means a special, unconditional love.

1) Love that comes from a pure heart

How can we have a pure heart? Ask of God. David prayed in Psalm 51:10 (KJV), "Create in me a clean heart, O God; and renew a right spirit within me."

2) Love that comes from a clear conscience

This seems impossible, but it's not. Recognize that condemnation is not from God but from the devil. Repent, turn from your sin, and move forward.

> There is therefore now no condemnation to them which are in Christ Jesus.
>
> —Romans 8:1 (KJV)

3) A love that comes from a genuine faith

In order to be filled with true love, we must believe in God. Have faith in God.

> But without faith it is impossible to please him: for he that cometh to God must believe that he is, and that he is a rewarder of them that diligently seek him.
>
> —Hebrews 11:6 (KJV)

Feel God's love today!

How can something as simple as love be the answer?

Read 1 Corinthians 1:27:

> But God hath chosen the foolish things of the world to confound the wise.

2 Corinthians 1:12:

> For our rejoicing is this, the testimony of our conscience, that in simplicity and godly sincerity, not with fleshly wisdom, but by the grace of God, we have had our conversation in the world, and more abundantly to you-ward.

> This is a trustworthy saying:
>
> If we die with him,
>
> We will also live with him.
>
> If we endure hardship,
>
> We will reign with him.
>
> If we deny him,
>
> He will deny us.
>
> If we are unfaithful,
>
> He remains faithful,
>
> For he cannot deny who he is.
>
> —2 Timothy 2:11–13 (NLT)

I have always been fond of this passage, especially the final stanza: "He remains faithful, for He cannot deny who He is." I am eternally grateful for a faithful God.

My husband made a statement one time when speaking to couples: "No one ever wants to hear, 'I'm faithful to my wife, most of the time.'"

"Most of the time" just isn't good enough. That fact is easy to recognize within the confines of a marriage, but just how faithful are we when it comes down to our relationship with God? Are we just faithful most of the time? Shame on us. What reassurance we have to know that even when "we are unfaithful, He remains faithful"!

Does God's unending faithfulness guarantee us a carefree, prosperous life? Not even a little bit. The Bible contains contingencies. Even the free gift of eternal life through Christ Jesus requires repentance on our part to receive. God laid out many marvelous blessings and promises for us, the faithful. Equivocally, God lists the warnings of what's to happen to us, the unfaithful. Mark His word; it will be as He has promised one way or the other.

Do not blame God. "He cannot deny who He is." His word will come to pass.

Will you be found faithful?

What does your faithfulness to God look like?

> So that all who trust in God will devote themselves to doing good.
>
> —Titus 3:8b (NLT)

What does it mean to do good? Is "good" subjective?

> Our people must learn to do good by meeting the urgent needs of others.
>
> —Titus 3:14 (NLT)

When we do good, we are unselfishly thinking of others. The act of doing good becomes second nature when practiced. Titus 3:14 says we "must learn to do good by...." We must take action. We must be about the practice of doing good, and the more we do good, the easier it will become.

Wave. Smile. Make eye contact. Greet a stranger. Slow down. Say, "I'm sorry." Think of others first. Be the last in line; somebody's got to do it. Empty the dishwasher. Take out the trash. Replace the liner. Say, "I love you." Say, "Jesus loves you." Do good.

My goofy thought:

Do good spelled backward is *Do☺ God!*

List some daily examples of how you can practice doing good:

> I, Paul, write this with my own hand: I will repay it. And I won't mention that you owe me your very soul!
>
> —Philemon 1:19 (NLT)

This short letter written to Philemon from Paul contains a story of second chances. History explains that Onesimus, as a slave, stole from his owner, Philemon, and ran away. Onesimus came to know Paul, and Paul introduced him to Jesus and a new life. Now that Onesimus has changed, Paul intends to send him back home, not as a fugitive slave, but as a redeemed brother in Christ.

It's comical to me. Apparently, Paul knows that Philemon has a past, too. Paul does not elaborate but simply reminds Philemon, "I won't mention that you owe me your very soul!" Like a line from a sitcom, Paul says he won't mention it—yet, in that very statement, he mentions it.

I'm certain Philemon's heart melted toward his runaway slave, Onesimus, once Paul reminded him of his own second chance. Not only was Onesimus to be allowed to return, but he was also to be elevated. Onesimus left a slave but returned a brother. What an amazing God we serve!

We serve a God of second chances, and third chances, and fourth chances.... The redeeming blood of Jesus and our step of faith is all it takes.

> I am praying that you will put into action the generosity that comes from your faith as you understand and experience all the good things we have in Christ.
>
> —Philemon 1:6 (NLT)

As you contemplate the redemptive power of Christ over your own life, name some people to whom you need to offer that same opportunity of redemption. Forgiveness truly is freeing.

Seeing then that we have a great high priest, that is past into the heavens, Jesus the Son of God, let us hold fast our profession. For we have not an high priest which cannot be touched with the feelings of our infirmities; but was in all points tempted like as we are, yet without sin. Let us therefore come **boldly** into the throne of grace, that we may obtain mercy, and find grace to help in time of need.

—Hebrews 4:14–16

I have heard thy prayer, I have seen thy tears: behold, I will heal thee: ...And I will add unto thy days fifteen years.

—2 Kings 20:5b–6a (the story of King Hezekiah)

Malachi 3:6 tells us a wonderful promise from God: "For I am the Lord, I change not." God is. We can hold fast to everything He has ever promised. Hebrews 6:18 tells us it is impossible for God to lie. God fulfills His every promise through His son, Jesus.

Having stated this truth that God does not change, I would build your confidence and faith by telling you that God can and does change His mind. Never confuse these two statements. James 5:16b: "The effectual fervent prayer of a righteous man availeth much." You are not stuck in your present situation. Destiny has not dealt you an evil hand. Stop moping and start praying!

Hezekiah turned to God, and God answered! Your prayers matter; my prayers matter; our prayers make a difference to God.

Pray with boldness and faith today. Seek the face of God. He will hear. He will answer. God is good. God is love. His character never changes, yet His mercies are new every morning.

Hebrews is filled with examples of faith. Read chapter 11 today. It's known as "the faith chapter."

> Let there be tears for what you have done. Let there be sorrow and deep grief. Let there be sadness instead of laughter, and gloom instead of joy.
>
> —James 4:9 (NLT)

How encouraging is this verse? *Not!* But I like this verse anyway because it's a clear picture of what repentance should look like.

I'm reminded of King Josiah of the Old Testament. His father had done evil in the sight of the Lord, put up false gods, and taken away the scrolls of God's Holy Word. Josiah became king when he was only eight years old. Can you imagine? But Josiah did right in the sight of the Lord. (I'm thinking Josiah had a pretty good mama.) One day, the high priest found the book of the law and had the court secretary read it to the king.

> When the king heard what was written in the Book of the Law, he tore his clothes in despair.
>
> —2 Kings 22:11 (NLT)

Josiah recognized the sin all of Israel was committing. He outwardly repented with sorrow; then he sought the Lord. King Josiah destroyed all the places of pagan worship and commanded all of the people to repent and change their ways.

Repentance begets change. Repentance is more than saying, "I'm sorry." Repentance requires that you stop the sin and commit it no more.

There is good news. Once you repent, you can remove your torn mourning clothes and don your party outfit.

> He will give a crown of beauty for ashes, a joyous blessing instead of mourning, festive praise instead of despair. In their righteousness, they will be like great oaks that the Lord has planted for his own glory.
>
> —Isaiah 61:3 (NLT)

Pour out your heart before the Lord today. Journal to Him a prayer of repentance.

> Give all your worries and cares to God, for He cares about you.
>
> —1 Peter 5:7 (NLT)

> Consider the lilies of the field, how they grow; they toil not, neither do they spin: and yet I say unto you, that even Solomon in all his glory was not arrayed like one of these. Wherefore, if God so clothes the grass of the field, which today is, and tomorrow is cast into the oven, shall He not much more clothe you, O ye of little faith?
>
> —Matthew 6:28b–30 (KJV)

My daughter and I made a twenty-four-hour trip simply to see the Texas wildflowers blooming alongside the roadway. Naturally, we threw in some eating and shopping along the way. We took our time, and on more than one occasion, we stopped and took advantage of the picturesque views.

Jesus said, "Consider the lilies." I can imagine if Jesus was from central Texas, He might have said, "Consider the bluebonnets."

As I gaze upon a field of wildflowers, I marvel at the beauty and contrast. Bluebonnets, Indian paintbrushes, and buttercups are a few of my childhood favorites. Each flower is unique in color and form, yet together, they create a beautiful blanket for the earth.

Jesus said of the Father, "Shall He not much more clothe you?" Why is it so difficult to place our trust in God? He proves himself season after season. God's got this! He clothes the flowers, and He will clothe me.

1 Peter 5:7 assures me I am what God cares about! He cares for me. The word *care* in the Greek means "to be of interest or concern." God is concerned about me. God is interested in me.

All the cares, worries, and anxieties I have in this world are no match for my God. I must give my cares to Him. You must give your cares to Him. For He cares for me, and He cares for you!

List your cares:

Now, pray and ask God to lift the burden that accompanies these cares and burdens.

> In view of all this, make every effort to respond to God's promises. Supplement your faith with a generous provision of moral excellence, and moral excellence with knowledge, and knowledge with self-control, and self-control with patient endurance, and patient endurance with godliness, and godliness with brotherly affection, and brotherly affection with love for everyone. The more you grow like this, the more productive and useful you will be in your knowledge of our Lord Jesus Christ.
>
> —2 Peter 1:5–8 (NLT)

Whew! That's quite a list. It is my desire to be more productive and useful in my knowledge of Jesus, so I must make the effort.

Let's examine the qualities in list form:

Faith

Moral excellence

Knowledge

Self-control

Patient endurance

Godliness

Brotherly affection

Love

We begin with faith.

> For ye are all the children of God by faith in Christ Jesus.
>
> —Galatians 3:26

We believe because we have faith. But as in any good diet, we must add supplements.

The first supplement needed is moral excellence: the quality of doing what is right and avoiding what is wrong.

To moral excellence we must add knowledge: the state of knowing. Proverbs 2:6 explains, "For the Lord giveth wisdom: out of his mouth cometh knowledge and understanding." If you spend time in God's word, your knowledge will increase.

To knowledge we add self-control: by your own will, you control your emotions, desires, and actions. Proverbs 12:23 warns us, "A prudent man concealeth knowledge: but the heart of fools proclaimeth foolishness." We must exercise self-control as we interact with others.

Patient endurance supplements self-control. I love this definition of *patient*: "bearing or enduring pain, difficulty, provocation, or annoyance with calmness."

To that add godliness: being a godly person. 1 Peter 1:16 states, "Be ye holy, as I am holy." Every day, we must work to be more like Christ.

To godliness we need to add a healthy dose of brotherly affection. I think this is best described in 1 Corinthians 12:25: "That there should be no schism in the body; but that the members should have the same care one for another." Show a loyalty and affection toward others as if they are part of you because we all comprise the body of Christ.

To sum up 1 Corinthians 13, without love I am nothing, so it makes perfect sense that the final ingredient in our list is love.

(All definitions in this excerpt come from freedictionary.com.)

Reexamine 2 Peter 1:5–8.

List the areas upon which you need to improve. Brainstorm some ways to be more productive and useful.

> This is real love—not that we loved God, but that He loved us and sent His Son as a sacrifice to take away our sins.
>
> —1 John 4:10 (NLT)

Please, please, please take time today to read the passage 1 John 4:7–21.

If only I possessed the talent necessary to adequately compose a description of the revelation of God's love I so strongly felt in service yesterday morning, then perhaps you, too, could bask in His life-changing, unrelenting love. I will attempt to relive the moment with these mere words on a page. Imagine you are in attendance.

Sunday morning praise flows smoothly. The crowd seems a bit low today; perhaps the threat of rain kept some people home this morning, although the only raindrops came in a brief afternoon shower. Speaking of rain, Jeannie begins worship service describing her Saturday night dream. With emotions high in her voice, she pushes through the tears to share her experience: "I stood to lead worship, and the children flooded the altar area without prompting, and soon all of the adults followed. The altar was filled with people. Everyone was shoulder to shoulder, too many to count. I looked out over the crowd, and it began to rain. I could hardly see, for the rain was falling so heavily, saturating everyone."

Wow! Such a powerful dream! I am so glad Jeannie shared.

Our first worship song, "Jesus, We Love You" by Bethel Music, feels easy and joyful, as if we are singing our very own love story to Jesus. The song ends; the presence of the Lord blankets us in warmth. Something shifts. Instead of transitioning into the next prepared song, Elias begins singing "Oh, How He Loves Us" by David Crowder Band.

> "He loves us!
>
> Oh, how
>
> He loves us..."

I'm overwhelmed. It's so simple, yet it changes everything. "He loves me. Oh, how He loves me." Regardless of anything I've done or could ever do, God loves me.

The revelation of God's unconditional love changes everything! Because He first loved me, I learn how to love Him, how to love others. Because He loves me, I desire to please Him and live my life for Him. Because He loves me, I am changed.

I know the scriptures by heart. I am taught of God's love. But the overwhelming flood of assurance, just like the rain in Jeannie's dream, washed over me in a new way Sunday morning. I experienced love from the inside out, and you can, too.

Take time to read 1 John, listen to David Crowder sing "Oh, How He Loves Us" on YouTube, and invite the presence of God to shower you with His love.

2 John 1:1–13

You must read the entire book. Only thirteen verses long. How have I never paid attention to verse 1?

> The elder unto the elect lady and her children.

John, at this point in his life, called himself "elder." Most of the apostles had been martyred, as the years passed; he indeed was an elder.

But what struck me the most interesting today is the fact that John wrote to a lady. I did some research, and we don't know who the lady is, but she must be a prominent figure for him to call her "elect lady." Wikipedia alludes to the possibility of the term *lady* referring to a church body. Regardless of the actual recipient over two thousand years ago, I receive John's message loud and clear.

Verse 6a: "And this is love, that we walk after his commandments."

Verse 10: "If there come any unto you, and bring not this doctrine [of Christ], receive him not."

Second John gives us a strong warning to follow after Jesus's commandments and to avoid false teachings.

Can you think of present-day false teachings? How might we avoid being confused and led astray?

> Beloved, I wish above all things that thou mayest prosper and be in health, even as thy soul prospereth.
>
> —3 John 1:2

The soul comes first. Our innermost thoughts, feelings, and beliefs toward God must be our priority. How I aspire to be described as Gaius is in verse 5: "Thou doest faithfully whatsoever thou doest to the brethren, and to strangers"! I desire to extend to all people the love of Christ.

Third John reads quickly. Take time today to read the letter as if it were written directly to you. Do the attributes of Gaius hold true for you and your Christian walk?

Jude

The book of Jude begins with quite a warning. Jude reminds us of the mercy and wrath of God. Even as God brought deliverance time and again to the children of Israel, destruction also fell upon those who did not believe. In verses 17–18, Jude warns, "Remember...how they told you there [would] be mockers...who...walk after their own ungodly lusts."

We, too, must be reminded that we live in a sinful world. Those who refuse Jesus mock and scorn the righteous. I encourage you not to lose heart.

> But ye, beloved, building yourselves on your most holy faith, praying in the Holy Ghost, keep yourselves in the love of God, looking for the mercy of our Lord Jesus Christ unto eternal life.
>
> —Jude 1:20–21

Say a special prayer today. Ask the Lord to lift your spirits.

Revelation.

This book is full of mysteries. Even in that, we can find nuggets of truth and encouragement for our future! Our eternity with God!

Chapter 1, verse eight, proclaims, "I am the Alpha and the Omega—the beginning and the end, says the Lord God. I am the one who is, who always was, and who is still to come—the Almighty One."

I encourage you to read all of chapter 2 and chapter 3. The Lord speaks to the churches. You will find that there are good and there are bad things about each one. Aren't we thankful that the Lord sees our good and impresses upon us those areas in which we need to improve? He does not hide His will from us. He shows us what we should do in order to follow Him better.

We live to die. The apostle Paul says it best: "To live is Christ and to die is gain" (Philippians 1:21 KJV).

> They were amazed at his teaching, for he taught as one who had real authority—quite unlike the teachers of religious law.
>
> —Mark 1:22

> And Jesus came and spake unto them saying, All power is given unto me in heaven and earth.
>
> —Matthew 28:18

How could Jesus teach with such authority? Because He indeed had authority. Sadly, the spiritual leaders of the time had no authority because pride, arrogance, and self-sufficiency had replaced humility, compassion, and desire for the presence of God.

Pride.

The religious leaders did not recognize Jesus as the Messiah because they did not need a Messiah. They had already arrived. These men knew the law; they had easy access to the written word of the prophets.

> The pride of thine heart hath deceived thee.
>
> —Obadiah 1:3

> Pride goeth before destruction, and an haughty spirit before a fall. Better it is to be of an humble spirit with the lowly.
>
> —Proverbs 16:18–19

These leaders refused to be grouped among the lowly and even went so far as to mock Jesus for His acquaintance with such people.

Jesus, on the other hand, spoke of Himself in this way: "Take my yoke upon you, and learn of me; for I am meek and lowly in heart: and ye shall find rest unto your souls" (Matthew 11:29).

Paul speaks of Jesus in his letter to the Philippians 2:7–8:

> But [Jesus] made himself of no reputation and took upon him the form of a servant, and was made in the likeness of men: and being found in fashion as a man, he humbled himself, and became obedient unto death, even the death of the cross.

Arrogance:

> But the Pharisees said, "He casteth out devils through the prince of the devils."
>
> —Matthew 9:34

Pharisees questioned why Jesus ate with sinners (Matthew 9:11); why they fasted yet the disciples did not (Matthew 9:14); why the disciples plucked corn on the Sabbath (Matthew 12:1); why Jesus healed on the Sabbath (Matthew 12:10). They sought a sign (Matthew 12:38); wondered why the disciples didn't wash their hands (Matthew 15:2); tried to trick Jesus concerning the law (Matthew 19:3). Many times, questioning the word of God from prophets of old, the Pharisees and Sadducees would try to trick Jesus (Matthew 22).

With all of these things, the religious leaders attempted to discredit Jesus and at the same time build themselves up as superior in the eyes of the people. The people, however, longed for a savior. The people needed saving. The compassion Jesus showed brought healing, forgiveness, companionship, and a sense of belonging. Jesus enabled the common man to seek the face of God again and not depend on others.

Matthew 16:24, John 7:37: "If any man…come…."

Self-sufficiency:

All these years, the people had to bring their offerings to the religious leaders to make atonement to God for sin. We know how the sacrifices became not much of a sacrifice at all but were provided for purchase at the temple gate. These leaders considered themselves to be the closest to God on earth. They knew all of the scriptures and prophecies of old. They wore the priestly garments and stayed at the temple. They kept the law, with ritual, so all could see; yet, they had no authority.

Why? Because they did not "know" God. They had no intimate relationship with the Father; thus they could not recognize the Son. They had no love (1 Corinthians 13:1–2).

Jesus, on the other hand, never gloried in the miracles but gave all of the glory to His Heavenly Father (John 5:18–47, John 8:13–19, 28–29). Jesus continuously sought the face of God (Luke 2:46, Luke 4:1–14, Luke 4:42, Luke 5:16, Luke 6:12, Luke 9:10, Luke 9:28–36, Luke 22:39–47, Luke 23:34, 46).

Jesus sought the face of His Father, seeking to do His perfect will, even unto death!

I want to end with this special quote from Revelation 21:3–5 (NLT):

> I heard a loud shout from the throne saying, "Look, God's home is now among his people! He will live with them, and they will be his people. God himself will be with them. He will wipe every tear from their eyes, and there will be no more death or sorrow or crying or pain. All these things are gone forever." And the one sitting on the throne said, "Look, I am making everything new!" And then he said to me, "Write this down, for what I tell you is trustworthy and true."

Let Jesus make you new today!